Nelson Guide to

2003–2004

Grant Heckman

University of New Brunswick
at Saint John

THOMSON

NELSON

Australia   Canada   Mexico   Singapore   Spain   United Kingdom   United States

NELSON
THOMSON LEARNING™

Nelson Guide to Web Research 2003–2004
by Grant Heckman

Editorial Director and Publisher:
Evelyn Veitch

Executive Editor:
Chris Carson

Marketing Manager:
Cara Yarzab

Developmental Editor:
Alwynn Pinard

Production Editor
Carrie Withers

Production Coordinator:
Helen Locsin

Copy Editor and Proofreader:
Gilda Mekler

Art Director:
Ken Phipps

Cover Image and Design:
Anne Bradley

Compositor:
Andrew Adams

Printer:
Webcom

National Library of Canada Cataloguing in Publication Data

Heckman, Grant, 1955–
    Nelson guide to Web research, 2003–2004 / Grant Heckman.

ISBN 0-17-622387-8

1. Computer network resources. 2. Internet searching. 3. Web search engines. I. Title. II. Title: Guide to Web research, 2003–2004.

ZA4226.H425 2003
025.04   C2003-900183-0

Contents

Foreword

The *Nelson Guide to Web Research 2003–2004* is intended to supply some strategies and contexts for students who use the Internet as an academic resource. It refers the reader to many useful Web sites on a variety of topics related to academic writing and research.

A basic working knowledge of the computer is assumed—for example, the ability to gain access to the Internet and to perform rudimentary word-processing tasks. As a result of this assumption, dictated in part by limitations of space, very little specific technical instruction is supplied. This information is very easy to find elsewhere—indeed, it is almost always on the computer itself, in its Help files.

The Internet can be a daunting environment for the relative newcomer, and it has its hazards for all online researchers. However, once you have mastered a few basic techniques and crucial tools, you can move quickly and efficiently to useful information, which is precisely what this book is intended to help you do.

Introduction

THE NATURE AND ORGANIZATION OF THE INTERNET

The Internet is a global system of computer networks, in which millions of machines are linked together by systems of common commands. The World Wide Web (WWW) is a network of servers that uses a particular protocol to share hypertext data and resources. (Hypertext is a form of text that contains links to other texts; it also makes possible the transfer of digitized images and sound files and supports real-time interactive communication.) The Web has become one of the most popular ways of using the Internet, and as a result the two terms are now used more or less synonymously. The Web is growing unimaginably quickly; it is the most vast, uncontrolled, elusive body of information that has ever existed, and it constitutes a revolution in the portability and accessibility of knowledge potentially even more far-reaching than the invention of the printing press. More than three billion Web pages exist in a largely unregulated system within which people are making things up as they go along. This situation, unique in human history, presents students with an entirely new and constantly changing set of possibilities and problems.

THE STRENGTHS AND LIMITATIONS OF THE INTERNET AS A RESEARCH TOOL

Some people believe that the Internet will eventually contain all of human knowledge. If this happens, it won't be anytime soon (as anyone who has spent a fruitless hour trying to find something online will tell you). Although the amount of academic information on the Internet is large and increasing rapidly, it still represents a tiny fraction of the resources that are available elsewhere in other forms. At the moment, then, for most students, the Internet should be considered a secondary resource after the library, which still contains the most useful, reliable, and easily accessible materials.

The Internet does, however, have some obvious advantages over any print medium. One of these advantages is speed: ideas, images, and sounds can be disseminated around the world in seconds. This makes it ideally suited to contain the most up-to-date information available, and it often does. New knowledge in a particular field can appear on the Internet far more quickly than it can appear in a book, although this efficiency comes at a price. Material on the Internet is fluid; unlike the content of a book, information on the Internet may not be the same tomorrow, if indeed it is there at all. Also, there is more onus placed on the researcher to evaluate the quality and integrity of material encountered on the Internet. Anyone can post anything online; the mechanisms of control and assessment that usually apply to other academic materials do not necessarily apply to online information. This being said, the majority of the Web sites that are useful to student researchers are connected to reputable academic, government, or other institutions, and although these resources are still necessarily less stable and dependable than printed matter, they can be used with some confidence.

One of the Internet's problems, paradoxically, is the rapid increase in the amount of information it makes available and the resulting difficulty of efficiently organizing and navigating that information. The Internet is in some ways getting more cumbersome and harder to use effectively, a reality that every researcher who turns to it will encounter at some time or another. Internet watchers have recently also turned their attention to the "invisible" or "deep" Web, a vast collection of databases and transitory information that is usually inaccessible to conventional search tools and therefore largely unexploited.

The Internet is great for statistics, weak on historical literary criticism, effective for general reference, weak on specialized political theory, and so on; users who approach the Internet with the basic tools and strategies that follow will quickly discover both its wonders and its limitations for their own purposes.

Chapter 1

Finding Information

■■■■ UNDERSTANDING URLS

Every Web site has an address, called a URL (uniform resource locator). Like a street address on a letter, which presents its component parts in a standardized way, a URL follows a fixed pattern and order, and it becomes progressively more specific as it proceeds. Here is a sample:

http://www.nelson.com/college/question.html

protocol   server domain domain type   directory path

The first part of the address, the protocol, specifies the type of resource or the method of access.

- **http://** stands for "hypertext transfer protocol" and provides access to a Web site. **Note:** It is no longer necessary to include this protocol when inputting a Web address in most browsers.

Other types of Internet resources have their own identifying protocols, which must always be specified:

- **telnet://** provides access to another computer's login screen
- **news://** provides access to a newsgroup
- **ftp://** stands for file transfer protocol and provides access to files
- **file://** gives access to a specific file

The second part of the address (**www.nelson.com**) contains the server (**www**) and the domain (**nelson**), a unique name identifying whose site it is. The second part of the domain, the domain type (**.com**), tells you what kind of site it is or where it is from:

- **.com** commercial
- **.edu** educational institution (U.S.)
- **.org** organization (usually a not-for-profit group)
- **.net** networking
- **.gov** government (U.S.)
- **.mil** military (U.S.)
- **.ca** from Canada (there are similar short forms for other countries, such as **.au** for Australia)

These domain types are now proliferating as a result of the dramatic increase in the number of sites on the Internet—it is like adding new area codes to a phone system. Some of the recent additions include **.museum**, **.biz** and **.info**.

If the URL continues beyond this point, the rest of the address (**college/question.html**) is the directory path within the site, which in some cases includes subpaths that identify specific file names. In our example, **college** is the initial directory path and **question.html** specifies a single file within it, **html** being an initialism for "hypertext mark-up language").

PLANNING AND REFINING A SEARCH

One of the most common complaints about the Internet is that it is difficult to zero in quickly on relevant material. A mind-boggling glut of information exists on the Internet, and people find themselves wading through screen after screen of material that is of no use to them, which is time-consuming and frustrating. To overcome this problem, you must learn how to plan and refine your search. To do this, you need to know which tools are available and how to make them work for you.

Search engines and directories are the two most common means of finding information on the Internet. A search engine scans millions of Web pages for the presence of keywords, links, and other information; you ask it to find information on, say, Shakespeare, and its Web-crawling software examines the Web sites in its database, almost instantly returning a list of "hits," or links to sites. Directories, on the other hand, organize an edited collection of Web sites by subject. Using a directory to find information on Shakespeare, you select the "Literature" option from a menu category entitled "Arts and Humanities," and then perhaps the option "Criticism and Theory" from the subsequent menu, and so on, until you end up with a series of Web pages devoted to the specific aspect of Shakespeare you are exploring.

The distinction between these two tools is now somewhat blurred: most search engines have some sort of directory on their home page, and most major directories now offer the option of keyword searches of the Internet. Still, each method of searching has its own advantages and disadvantages.

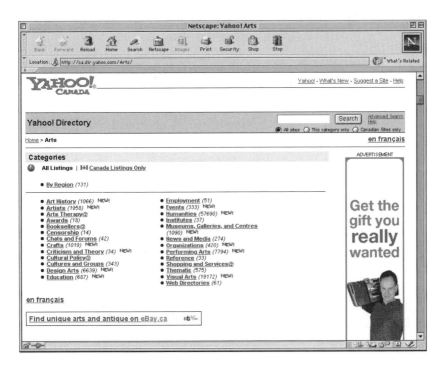

This screen shot depicts Yahoo's initial Arts menu, which offers various arts-related search topics and access to subject-specific directories.

Screen capture courtesy of Yahoo Canada.

SEARCH ENGINES

The key to using a search engine efficiently is to construct a specific and limiting sequence of keywords that will produce a manageable number of relevant, useful hits. It also helps to have some idea of how individual search engines index the Web and what sort of database each one is searching. Every search engine has a Help file, which provides all the information necessary to tailor sophisticated searches. *Read these pages!* They explain the special features and protocols of the particular engine and help you get the most out of it. This will save you time in the long run. All search engines also have an advanced search option designed to make the refining of searches easy and efficient. These advanced search options are all set up slightly differently; try a few of them to see which work best for you.

Some of the most useful techniques for refining your searches are described below.

BOOLEAN OPERATORS

The use of Boolean operators simply involves inserting "and," "or," or "not" between keywords to narrow a search and eliminate irrelevant material.

- (Keyword 1) *and* (Keyword 2) means find only entries that include both of these words.

- (Keyword 1) *not* (Keyword 2) means find entries containing Keyword 1 but not Keyword 2.

- (Keyword 1) *or* (Keyword 2) means find entries that contain either word.

Greater specificity of keyword commands has dramatic results in separating the wheat from the chaff. A search on the search engine AltaVista using only the keyword "Shakespeare" yields a somewhat unwieldy 1 665 601 hits. If you're looking for information specifically on Shakespeare's sonnets, for example, you could instead enter "Shakespeare and sonnets," which produces 35 326 hits. "Shakespeare and sonnets and 'dark lady'" returns 921 sites. Adding other keywords that narrow the search even further will usually result in still fewer hits; even if it doesn't, it will generally move the most relevant sites closer to the top of your search results. (**Note:** Your keywords do not have to fit in the window into which you insert them; you can input as many as you like.)

PHRASES

If you type in as your keywords "Karl Marx," the search engine will return some hits involving only "Karl," and some involving only

"Marx," including material about the comedian Groucho and the pop singer Richard, among others. If, however, you enclose "Karl Marx" in quotation marks, the search engine will look only for the two words together and in that order. Any time you want your keywords considered as a phrase rather than as a list of individual terms, you need to enclose them in quotation marks.

Search engines ignore minor words such as "the" and "in"; they are called "stop words," and any given search engine may be programmed to discount as many as 200 of them. Including such minor words in a phrase with quotation marks ensures that they will be part of your search. (Alternatively, placing an "and" or "+" before such words will also include them in your search.)

WILDCARDS (TRUNCATION)

If you place an asterisk (*) at the end of a string of letters, most search engines will seek out all the variations that begin with that string; for example, if you type "Canad*" the search engine will look for "Canada," "Canadian," "Canadians," and so on. You can also place an asterisk in the middle of a word so that the search will include more than one spelling of that word: using "hon*r," for example, will generate a search for both "honor" and "honour." Truncation can also be used to include plural forms in your search: typing "habitat*" will return results containing both "habitat" and "habitats." Though most search engines support this type of search, there is some variation in the commands.

PROXIMITY OPERATORS

Some search engines allow you to specify how close keywords should be to each other using a "near" command. The distance between terms can often be adjusted from a few words to a page or more. Such a command has many uses. For example, if you initiate a search for "Susannah near Moodie," the search engine will return pages that include "Susannah Moodie" and also—because you have included the command "near," and therefore not specified an order—those that include "Moodie, Susannah."

PARENTHESES (NESTING)

Within Boolean strings, elements can be grouped into intelligible units, or chunks, by the use of parentheses. Some search engines treat the resulting unit like an algebraic parenthesis: they execute whatever is within the parentheses first. Other engines treat parentheses much like quotation marks.

MAJOR DIFFERENCES BETWEEN SEARCH ENGINES

Ranking of Findings: The main criteria for the ranking of a search engine's findings are the frequency and location of keywords, but because there are other variations in individual programs, **the same query will elicit a different set of responses from every search engine.** Some search engines weigh the popularity of sites or the number of links to certain sites in their ranking, the idea being that users have "voted" for these sites and thus confirmed their quality.

Paid Listings: Most search engines have always sold advertising, in the form of banners and sidebars on the margins of their search results; most now also offer "paid inclusion" or "paid placement." Paid listings appear first, and are usually given a euphemistic title, such as "sponsored matches." They are followed by the results based solely on your keywords, which will be in a separate section, sometimes set off graphically or with a new font or a heading such as "Web results." For researchers, this second set of results will in most cases be more relevant and useful.

Boolean Operators: Most search engines support the use of the basic Boolean operators, but the details of the commands vary somewhat. Some search engines, for example, allow the use of symbols such as + and - ; some will recognize "not"; some will recognize only "and not"; and so on. Several search engines have advanced search menus that enable you to perform Boolean searches and other search variations by just clicking your mouse on menus or boxes.

Search Method: Some search engines scan only titles, summaries, meta-tags, or indexes; others, such as AltaVista, scan whole pages of text.

Databases: Each search engine has its own database, and these vary dramatically in size. Google scans more than 3 billion pages, whereas AltaVista indexes about 550 million. These numbers are constantly increasing as the Internet grows and as new technologies come into use. Although these databases necessarily overlap, they are all unique, and you may discover that particular search engines consistently return more useful results in your subject area.

Displaying of Results: Search engines typically return results in declining order of relevance to your query; most present you with summaries of sites they have found or with the first few sentences of the text, and some offer only titles. Some search engines allow you to choose how many hits per page you want to view or to customize the displaying of your results in other ways.

Case Sensitivity: Some search engines are case sensitive. This means that if you capitalize keywords, the engine will seek only cases that are capitalized the same way; if you leave your keywords in lowercase letters, the engine will seek both capitalized and lowercased instances of the words.

Each search engine's particular rules and methods are presented in its Help pages and "About Us" pages, and in its advanced search option.

FEATURES AND CHARACTERISTICS OF VARIOUS SEARCH ENGINES

The technologies employed by search engines change frequently; features such as speed of operation, size of databases, and types of services offered are in constant flux. As the Web matures, the major search engines are becoming increasingly similar and interconnected. As a result of the licensing and sharing of technologies, a single search on a single search engine may involve results from a number of different search engines and directories. The edited site collections of the directories LookSmart and Open Directory are used by a number of major search engines, for example, and searches on Yahoo! refer to the database of Google. Nevertheless, each search engine still has its own style, layout, database, and distinctive collection of search options, and frequent users of the Internet develop preferences according to the type of search they wish to perform.

There are Web sites devoted to search engines, such as Search Engine Watch (**www.searchenginewatch.com**) and Search Engine Showdown (**www.notess.com/search**), that offer advice on searches, reviews of search engines and directories, statistics on their size and performance, and links to search tools worldwide. The best way to keep up with changes, however, is to visit and use the various search engines yourself.

Google

www.google.com

- is a fast, efficient search engine with an immense database of more than 3 billion pages
- evaluates sites based on the number and nature of links that point to them, as well as on the presence of keywords
- offers a "similar pages" search with each hit
- searches images, groups (Newsgroups), directories, news and U.S. government sites as well as the Web

- applies its search technology to Open Directory's collection of sites
- allows you to limit searches according to language, domain, and location of keywords (e.g., in the site's title, URL, etc.)

All-the-Web

www.alltheweb.com

- searches a database of more than 2 billion documents
- searches mp3 and ftp files as well as Web sites, news, pictures, and videos
- supports customization of searches and display
- updates its pages every 11 days (vs. 28 for Google)
- analyses language patterns and identifies common phrases in keyword strings

AltaVista

www.altavista.com

- offers a *Prisma* search feature, which generates keywords related to your search that can be added to or substituted for your initial search terms with the click of a mouse
- offers extensive search options, including language, location, date of modification, topic, and multimedia
- allows you to customize your results display, offering links to related sites, date of most recent modification, size of site, etc.
- searches images, audio, video, directories, and news
- can translate pages into or out of a number of languages; these translations are done by a software program, not by a qualified human translator, and should be used only to glean a general idea of the content of a particular text (AltaVista also operates a free-standing—and free—all-purpose translation site called Babel Fish at **babelfish.altavista.com**)
- uses the LookSmart directory, customized by its own editors and algorithms

Lycos

www.lycos.com

- has a "fast forward" feature that allows you to split the screen and preview sites without clicking back and forth to results pages

- enables you to limit searches by language, specific fields (title, domain, URL), or links to particular sites
- offers a "second opinion" search with the same keywords on a selection of other search engines
- provides access to its version of Open Directory on its site map

There are many other useful general search engines, including the following:

Excite

www.excite.com

Teoma

www.teoma.com

METASEARCH TOOLS

Metasearch tools enable you to conduct a search on a number of search engines simultaneously. This has the obvious advantage of increasing the size of the database you are consulting. On the down side, such searches often are much slower than those conducted using a single search engine. (Some metasearch engines allow you to specify how long you are willing to wait for results.) Using multiple search engines can also degrade your search in a number of ways. For example, as we have seen above, the different search engines use different commands. Generally, if you submit to a metasearch engine a detailed query that does not conform to the rules of one—or more—of the individual search engines it consults, that search engine might change (default) your terms to others that may not correspond to your intentions (e.g., an "and" might become an "or"), thereby diluting your search. Remember also that metasearch engines return only a fraction of the results from each search engine they use.

Meta-search engines do have their uses. They can be used at the beginning of a major project to compare the kinds of results returned by various individual search engines, which can give you a sense of each engine's performance, and possibly reveal a particular engine's suitability for your purposes. A search on a metasearch engine also provides the user with a better sense of the resources available across the Internet on a subject than does a single search on a single engine. The usual problem with Internet searches is getting the number of hits small enough to manage, but if you need to cast your net as widely as possible, these tools may be useful to you.

Ixquick

www.ixquick.com

- lets you jump directly to search engines whose results are particularly valuable
- translates searches into each search engine's syntax
- awards sites stars for each search engine that has placed them in its top ten returns, providing users with an instant popularity ranking
- eliminates duplicate sites

Search.com

www.search.com

- provides results from more than 1000 sources
- includes suggestions alongside your results for refining your search
- allows results to be sorted by source, relevance, or date
- offers customized searches, in which users specify categories and search engines

Metacrawler

www.metacrawler.com

- lets you specify maximum waiting time
- uses ten major search engines or any chosen combination of them
- will filter results according to specified domains, regions, or countries
- displays results sorted by relevance, site, or source

Dogpile

www.dogpile.com

- returns results grouped by individual search engine
- uses 15 general search engines and a number of specialty engines for images, news, audio, and other particular sorts of information
- allows users to customize searches
- provides users the option of resubmitting the search on the individual search engine that initially provides the best results

Ask Jeeves

www.askjeeves.com

- enables you to search by asking questions in natural language
- responds to the question you pose with a list of similar questions, from which you choose one to be answered
- displays, as part of its results, a list of related Web sites organized by search engine
- includes a directory that displays the popularity of various sites among users

Kartoo

www.kartoo.com

- presents results arranged graphically in a colour-coded matrix
- accepts natural language queries

DIRECTORIES

A directory organizes a body of Web sites (its database) by categories. The first choice of categories offered is the most general, and the successive menus become more and more specific as you narrow down the exact subject of your search. Often a screen will offer you both a choice of individual Web sites and the option of further refining your search by category.

Most directories allow you to search their databases by keyword and to pinpoint your search using the various techniques described above. Unlike the vast resources scanned by the relatively undiscriminating software of a search engine, the databases of directories are assembled by human choice; this means that they are more limited, but they are also likely higher in quality. Most directories are, however, programmed to revert to scanning the Web if they cannot find what you are seeking within their own database. Many people are increasingly turning to directories as the growth of the Web outstrips any search engine's ability to index effectively more than a fraction of the existing sites; users complain of "link rot," as search engines return ever-increasing numbers of often largely irrelevant hits.

Directories are often useful for getting a sense of the kind and depth of information available on a particular topic. This is especially true of specialized directories, of which there are thousands—there is one, for example, devoted to orchids! Such directories often provide an exhaustive and up-to-date account of the online materials available in a single area of inquiry.

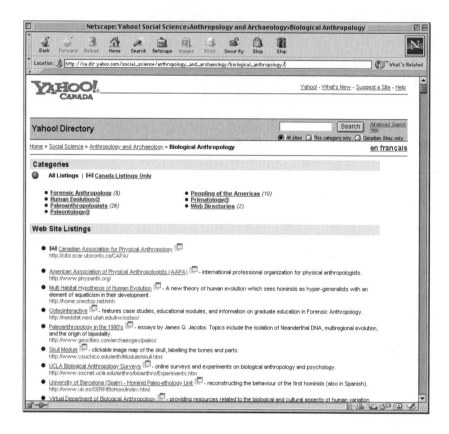

This screen shot depicts Yahoo's biological anthropology page which offers both annotated links to individual Web sites and a menu that includes more specific topics within the subject and anthropology-related Web directories.

Screen capture courtesy of Yahoo! Canada.

A reliable basic strategy for starting your research on a topic is to go first to a general directory, choose your broad area of inquiry, and then move on to the specialized directories that are almost always among the subcategories resulting from your initial choice.

GENERAL INTEREST DIRECTORIES

Yahoo!

www.yahoo.com

- is one of the most popular Web portals in the world

12

- allows you to search by category or by Web site
- employs 150 editors to manage its collection of more than 1.8 million sites
- offers "Yahoo picks" featuring new sites
- often provides, within category menus, links to other more specialized directories

Open Directory
dmoz.org

- appears similar in structure to Yahoo! but has a different database of more than 3.8 million sites
- uses more than 54 000 volunteer editors, each responsible for a particular topic, to index the Web and keep track of emerging and dead sites
- supports advanced searches and regional searches
- contains links to many other useful search tools
- provides directory results for Lycos and HotBot

LookSmart
www.looksmart.com

- employs 200 editors to manage a collection of 2.5 million sites
- uses the Inktomi search engine
- functions as a stand-alone directory, and also provides directory results for AltaVista, Excite, Netscape, and others

ACADEMIC DIRECTORIES

General interest directories such as Yahoo! are designed to cater to the needs of the public at large, and many of their resources facilitate the recreational rather than the academic use of the Internet. There are, however, a number of more scholarly directories whose databases are more likely to be of use to the researcher.

Librarians' Index to the Internet
lii.org

- originates from the Library of California
- contains a database of more than 10 000 sites that have been assessed by librarians for their academic value
- provides a weekly annotated list of new sites

Internet Public Library
www.ipl.org
- is a directory organized by librarians
- offers a "reference collection," which includes access to dictionaries, thesauruses, books of quotations, etc.
- contains an "online literary criticism collection," which provides links to thousands of articles and theses
- provides links to magazines and newspapers from around the world
- contains links to an online text collection of more than 20 000 titles

Virtual Library
www.vlib.org
- is a multidisciplinary academic directory
- uses a staff of volunteer experts to maintain indexes in the various subject categories
- has connected, individual Web pages devoted to specific subject areas, which are excellent starting points for research in those areas

Infomine
infomine.ucr.edu
- is subtitled "Scholarly Internet Resource Collections"
- was constructed by librarians at the University of California
- contains thousands of links to databases, listservs, journals, articles, books, and directories

BUBL LINK
bubl.ac.uk/link
- originates from the University of Strathclyde
- indexes a database of more than 12 000 academic sites
- contains both a subject tree for browsing and a keyword search

SPECIALIZED DIRECTORIES
Among the most helpful tools for the Internet researcher are specialized directories whose databases are focused on one field of study, or even on a specific subject within that field. There are also directories devoted to helping you retrieve particular kinds of information, such as articles in online journals. Here are a few useful sites:

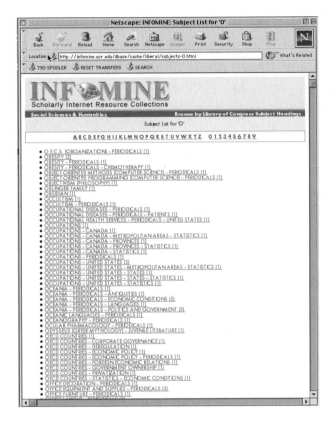

This screen shot from the humanities table of contents for the letter O from the Infomine site illustrates the vast number of links available on academic directories.

Screen capture courtesy of Infomine.

Social Science Information Gateway

sosig.ac.uk

- is a directory from Britain
- contains information at a high academic level
- provides extensive annotations for all links and includes a list of emerging resources

Humbul Humanities Hub

www.humbul.ac.uk

- is hosted by Oxford University and is a member of the same webring as SOSIG (above)

- focuses on British information and organizations, but provides access to international websites and resources

The British Academy Portal
www.britac.ac.uk/portal
- provides a directory of online resources in the humanities and social sciences

a grab-bag of (mainly) free bibliographies and bibliographic databases on the Web
www.leidenuniv.nl/ub/biv/freebase.htm#Par12
- provides links to free-access bibliographical information

Humanities Scholarship
www.wam.umd.edu/~mlhall/scholarly.html
- contains links to humanities scholarship arranged by time period, as well as information on computing, conferences, and university departments

A list of subject-specific directories is presented in Chapter 5.

FINDING CANADIAN SITES ON THE INTERNET

Most of the major search engines and directories have Canadian sites that feature Canadian news and information, and where you can search either only for Canadian sites, or within the entire Web, using the search engine's main database. (Note, however, that a "Canada only" search usually scans only Web sites that end in ".ca", thereby ignoring, for example, Canadian sites that end in ".com" and other domain types). Here are the addresses of a few of the major sites:

AltaVista Canada
ca-en.altavista.com

Yahoo! Canada
ca.Yahoo.com

Google Canada
www.google.ca

Sympatico/Lycos
pre.sympatico.ca

There are also some specifically Canadian search tools, including the following:

Canada.com

www.canada.com
- is a branch of the Southam newspaper chain
- searches Canadian sites or the entire Web, identifying Canadian sites with a Maple Leaf insignia
- gathers information from 30 Southam publications

Maple Square

www.maplesquare.com
- is a Canadian directory offering both browsing by subject categories and keyword searches
- accepts both formal and natural language searches

National Library of Canada – Canadian Information by Subject

www.nlc-bnc.ca/caninfo/ealpha.htm
- provides an extensive subject tree containing links to international Internet sites containing Canadian information

Canadian Databases

www.internets.com/scanada.htm
- contains a subject tree of Canadian and provincial databases
- offers keyword search of Agriculture Canada, Canadian Law, and other governmental information

SEARCH STRATEGIES

- Directories are a good place to begin if you want to browse and get a sense of what sorts of resources are available on a particular subject or within a particular category.
- Directory browsing can be useful in narrowing down a topic that is overly broad.
- General directories are often most useful in leading you to specialized directories in your subject areas, which will in turn lead to the actual Web sites you will find useful.

- If you know the precise focus of your subject, it is probably more efficient to go to a search engine.
- Be as precise and specific as possible in your choice of keywords and in the relationships you specify between them.
- At the beginning of a search, add keywords rather than substituting them; experienced researchers often employ keyword strings of four or five terms, or even more if necessary.
- Put the most important of your keywords first in any string. Some search engines weight keywords according to their order.
- Look for patterns in your results that can be addressed in your keyword strings. Could you eliminate some irrelevant hits by adding a term as a "not" command (so that the search engine will ignore pages containing that term)?
- Performing a search and scanning the first page or two of hits takes only a few seconds. Try a couple of searches with different combinations of keywords or different Boolean strings.
- Try one set of keywords with two or three different search engines.
- Try to match the kind of information you need with the strengths of the various search tools at your disposal; if you are looking for a very specific piece of information, for example, you will probably have more luck, and faster results, using a specialized directory than scrolling through the hundreds of hits returned by a metasearch engine.
- If the keywords you are using do not return the kind of materials you are looking for, try some synonyms or approach the question from another angle. Take a quick look at the most relevant site in your first results to see if it contains other keywords you might have missed.
- Take extra care typing in your keywords, and proofread them before you initiate the search. Your search can be affected by little details such as misspellings or variations in spelling, capitalization, accents, singulars and plurals, and so on. Human readers can correct tiny errors of these kinds and extract your intended meaning; computers cannot.
- If you are hopping from site to site exploring interesting links, bookmark sites that appear to be useful as you are passing through them. In a long session of searching, it's easy to lose

18

track of the location of sites you visit only momentarily. At the end of the session, take a few seconds to delete bookmarks you think you won't be using again; this guards against building up a huge list of bookmarks whose individual usefulness you will gradually forget.

- If you encounter a "File Not Found – 404" page, try trimming off part of the directory path of the URL (back to the previous slash "/"). Sometimes the link to a particular file is dead when the Web site is still functioning and has perhaps been reorganized. Trimming the URL in this way can also lead you to the homepage of an individual page you find useful, either to identify the sponsor/author of the site or to lead to other potentially relevant pages.

- Use, as a keyword phrase, fragments of text that you will be likely to find in the information you are looking for. For example, if you need to know the birth date of Picasso, type in as a keyword phrase "Picasso was born on"; the information you are seeking will often pop right up—sometimes on the results page itself.

- Keep track mentally of how long you spend on particular search initiatives and what kind of progress you make—be prepared to abandon fruitless searches that go on too long, and think in terms of other places you might find the needed material or possible changes of direction in your research.

- Be disciplined in terms of following interesting but irrelevant links—an hour can pass in the blink of an eye when you're surfing the Web.

Chapter 2

Resources

The domain name and the appearance of a Web site are the user's first clues as to its general usefulness as a research resource. The majority of Web sites are commercial—their domains end in ".com"—and it is good to remember that these sites exist principally to generate profits. (In fact, it is usually hard to forget this, as most of these sites are festooned with promotional material of every kind.) Many commercial sites are of value to researchers—all the major search engines are commercial enterprises, for example—but students will probably find that most usable academic information will be retrieved from sites with URLs ending in "ca," "org," "edu," "net," or "gov." The domain also identifies resources other than Web sites, such as email, listservs, and newsgroups.

LIBRARIES

Many of the sites called—or organized like—libraries on the Internet are really directories: they lead you and link you to information in other places rather than containing it themselves. Such sites include the Internet Public Library, the Virtual Library, and Infomine. However, most bricks-

and-mortar libraries—including major government collections, local public libraries, and the libraries of universities and colleges—can now also be accessed online; this usually means that it is possible to contact them and gain online access to their catalogues, although not yet to the full texts of most of the materials they contain. As with other areas of specialization, there are sites devoted to helping users locate and use library resources:

Libdex
www.libdex.com

- is an up-to-date commercial site of academic and public libraries
- allows you to browse 14 554 libraries

National Library of Canada
www.nlc-bnc.ca

- provides extensive links to Canadian libraries and much other information, especially governmental

Library of Congress
lcweb.loc.gov

- provides access to the catalogue of the library's own collection and links to U.S. government-related information

ELECTRONIC RESEARCH RESOURCES

One of the extraordinary things about the Internet is how much of it is free. Students should remember, however, that publishers and institutions are unlikely to give away material that they can sell; there is more academic information for sale or hire on the Web than there is available for free. Research conducted on the computer includes use of the many databases and fee-based online sources now available by subscription and in college and university libraries. Still, an ever-increasing amount of full-text material is available to all, and there are a number of sites on the Web designed to lead you to it.

FEE-BASED DATABASES

The bulk of many libraries' periodical and reference collections are now accessed online rather than on paper or microfilm. Each library has a unique collection of databases and services; your librarian, and probably also your library's own Web site, can acquaint you with your institution's particular resources. Individual users can also subscribe to many of these services. Here are a few examples of some common databases and the kinds of information they contain:

Infotrac®

infotrac.thomsonlearning.com

- a fully searchable online library containing complete articles from hundreds of scholarly and popular publications—journals, magazines, encyclopedias, and newsletters. The collection is broad and multidisciplinary. **NOTE:** A four-month subscription to Infotrac® is included in the purchase of many Nelson textbooks. See "Using Infotrac" below.

Canadian Business and Current Affairs (CBCE)

library.dialog.com/bluesheets/html/bl0262.html

- contains business and non-business journals and extensive Canadian information, such as the *Canadian Journal of Sociology* and *Quill and Quire*
- 30 percent of the journals within it are full text

Ebsco Host Databases

www-ca.ebsco.com/home/default.asp

- provides access to a number of scholarly databases—some, such as Academic Full Text Elite, are largely full text; others, such as Psych Info, provide abstracts and citations

Elsevier Science Server

www.elsevier.com

- provides full-text access to more than 100 journals, and access to the bibliographic databases Biobase, Embase, and Geobase

Project Muse

muse.jhu.edu

- provides full-text access to 40 journals from Johns Hopkins University Press and abstracts from 60 others, with an emphasis on the humanities

Ingenta

www.ingenta.com

- includes 5400 full-text online publications, as well as information from a total of 26 000 publications
- offers many links and some published material for free

Using Infotrac©

Infotrac is a database containing more than 12 million articles from more than 3000 publications. Articles can be read on screen, or printed, or emailed. The database includes articles dating back four years, and it is updated daily. Like other databases, Infotrac is a mini-Internet: you conduct keyword or subject searches that operate only within the collection of materials the database contains. A subject search assembles the articles from within the database relevant to your subject heading, arranging them by sub-topics; this introduces you to the available resources and helps you narrow your search. A keyword search isolates the articles that contain references to your subject; if your string of keywords is very specific, such a search will return only entries relevant to your narrowed sub-topic. Infotrac also offers a number of search options to further focus your keyword searches, such as name of journal, author, date, and so on.

Infotrac is very easy to use:

- Go to the Infotrac home page (infotrac.thomsonlearning.com).

- Enter your passcode into the login window (if it is your first visit, you will have to complete a registration screen before proceeding to the search page).

- Choose which kind of search you would like to begin with: subject guide or keyword.

- Type in your subject area/keywords and browse the returned list of articles.

- To bookmark an item within the site that interests you, click in the box entitled "Mark," which will add it to a list of relevant articles that you can return to at any time to access the item.

- To bring up the text of an article, click on "View text and retrieval choices." Many articles will start with an abstract, which will help you to decide whether the article is of use to you.

- To see an index of optional fields for enhanced searching, select "PowerTrac" on the initial search page.

FREE INTERNET RESOURCES

There are many full-text resources available for free on the Internet, and their number increases every month. Specialized directories in your field of inquiry will lead you to them. A number of Web sites exist to catalogue free online serials and other information sources. Here are a few of these:

Scholarly Journals Distributed Via the World Wide Web
info.lib.uh.edu/wj/webjour.html

Galileo Internet Resources
www.galileo.peachnet.edu

TUG Libraries
webdev.uwaterloo.ca/ejournals/index.html

JSTOR (JournalSTORage)
www.jstor.org

UNB Saint John Ward Chipman Library
www.unbsj.ca/library/serials/titles.htm

Many thousands of full-length texts are now available on the Internet, ranging from sophisticated, hyperlinked versions of the great classics to obscure books of non-fiction, fiction, and poetry. Here are a few of the major collections:

Bartleby.com
www.bartleby.com

- contains collections of fiction, non-fiction, and poetry, as well as many basic reference resources such as *Bartlett's Quotations*, *The Columbia Encyclopedia*, and *Fowler's Modern English Usage*

The Online Books Page
digital.library.upenn.edu/books

- contains 17 000 texts, news, and articles

Electronic Text Center Collections
etext.lib.virginia.edu/uvaonline.html

- contains 70 000 texts in 12 languages plus links to research resources

24

Humanities Text Initiative
ref.umdl.umich.edu
- includes several translations of the Bible and many public domain texts

Alex Catalogue of Electronic Texts
www.infomotions.com/alex
- a collection of public domain documents from American and English literature as well as Western philosophy

Project Gutenberg
www.promo.net/pg
- a collection of thousands of public domain texts, increasing at the rate of one a day

THE INVISIBLE WEB

The "invisible Web" (also called the "deep Web") is the body of Internet information that conventional search tools either choose not to index or are unable to index. Much of this information consists of either transitory files containing material such as stock prices and transportation schedules, or—of greater interest to the researcher—databases that are connected to the Internet but whose contents cannot be located and accessed using standard search engine keyword searches. Estimates of the size and importance of the invisible Web vary wildly, which suggests that, as with so many aspects of the Internet, no one really knows. A number of search tools that attempt to connect Internet users to some of this material have emerged, including the following:

Complete Planet
www.completeplanet.com

www.invisible-web.net
www.invisible-web.net

Flipper.com
www.flipper.com

IncyWincy
www.incywincy.com

Invisible Web.com
www.invisibleweb.com

GOVERNMENT INFORMATION

Most levels of government, as well as the departments and agencies within them, are now online; just about any government information you want can be had, and usually quickly. The sites are well linked, so it is easy to jump, for example, from the Government of Canada site to a provincial government site or to the Statistics Canada pages.

There are a number of Web sites devoted to helping you access government information.

CANADIAN

Canadian Government Information
www.nlc-bnc.ca/cangov/egovinfo.htm

Government of Canada
canada.gc.ca/main_e.html

National Archives of Canada
www.archives.ca

Statistics Canada
www.statcan.ca

INTERNATIONAL

Governments on the WWW
www.gksoft.com/govt

AMERICAN

Government Resources on the Web
www.lib.umich.edu/govdocs/govweb.html

Google U.S. Government Search
www.google.com/unclesam

Infomine (**infomine.ucr.edu**) and the Virtual Library (**www.vlib.org**) also have extensive links to government information, especially American.

LISTSERVS, NEWSGROUPS, CHATS, BLOGS, AND BULLETIN BOARDS

Listservs, newsgroups, chats, and bulletin boards are, apart from email, the principal interactive tools of the Internet. Unlike the one-way consumption involved in visiting a Web site, they enable ongoing two-way communication. Newsgroups are online discussion groups. Messages on a particular topic are posted publicly and are available to anyone who calls up the site, and everyone is free to respond. In the case of chats, users conduct a more or less real-time dialogue with one or more other people, whereas with newsgroups and bulletin boards, posted messages are responded to over a period of time. These forums are often unscreened; that is, there is no external control imposed on the content of anyone's contribution.

Listservs are interactive mailing lists. Messages on a certain topic are sent by email to a group of subscribers; individual subscribers can read the message and can choose to respond either to the entire group or solely to the author. Listservs are more regulated than are newsgroups; the content of listservs is usually monitored to prevent abusive messages or hate mail, and subscribers must apply for membership. Subscribers can often choose between receiving all messages, receiving a digest of the day's or week's messages, or receiving only an index from which they can choose which messages they would like to read.

Thousands of newsgroups and chats are essentially recreational, but well-chosen ones, as well as many listservs, can be of use to a researcher. They can provide a way to connect with people in your field, to encounter new ideas, and to be directed to new information. You can discuss a problem with fellow members of a group or enlist them to help you locate a piece of information; they are part of the human aspect of the hypertextual nature of the Internet. Listservs on very specific topics can provide an important—sometimes the only—regular source of new information.

You can locate newsgroups and listservs in a number of ways. Search engines devoted to groups may be found at many major portals, including Google and Yahoo (**groups.yahoo.com**). Once you get connected to specialized search engines and directories in your particular area of research, you will find information on more academic newsgroups and listservs popping up. Here are a few useful sites:

Directory of Scholarly and Professional E-Conferences
www.kovacs.com/directory

Tile.Net
tile.net

H-Net – Humanities and Social Sciences Online
www2.h-net.msu.edu

A recent addition to the formats of Internet information is the blog (short for "Weblog"), a kind of online diary whose entries often include links to other sites. Blogs began on personal Web sites, but academic variations are beginning to appear. Addresses for subject-specific blogs can now sometimes be found on academic sites alongside those of listservs and newsgroups. One source for research-related blogs is Library Weblogs (www.libdex.com/weblogs.html)

EMAIL

The most popular element of the Internet is electronic mail (email). Although email does not, for most people, bestow the same aesthetic pleasure as a handwritten letter by post, it has many advantages over conventional mail, some of them of interest to the researcher. It is much faster, obviously, and cheaper, especially in the case of international communication. It is also possible to send the same message instantly to a group of people, which can be useful if, for example, you wish to ask a number of people the same question. A particularly useful function is the attachment, which enables you to affix a word-processing file (or a scanned image, a sound file, etc.) to an email. Not surprisingly, email is the standard mode of communication among those online, and email addresses are often found on home pages, whereas normal mail ("snail mail") addresses may not be. These email addresses enable you to communicate with the creators of a Web site to assess their credibility, react to the site's content, or request further information.

An email address, like a URL, has standard component parts in a fixed order:

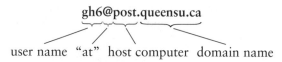

gh6@post.queensu.ca

user name   "at"   host computer   domain name

Many directories and search engines have an email address search option, and many provide email yellow pages, business and fax directories, and so on.

REFERENCE INFORMATION

There are many reference materials available free of charge on the Internet, from dictionaries and thesauruses to encyclopedias, style sheets, and language guides. These materials can be accessed in many ways. Major directories offer links to reference materials on their home pages, as do most online libraries (e.g., the Internet Public Library or the Virtual Library).

There are also a number of sites that specialize in resource material, such as refdesk.com (**www.refdesk.com**). There is even a search engine devoted to retrieving reference information: Search 22 (**www.search-22.com/reference.html**) offers a keyword search of 22 different reference sites and links to other resources.

INFORMATION ON ACADEMIC WRITING

Many universities and colleges have writing centres that have their own Web sites. A number of online writing labs (OWLs) offer the student writer handouts, links to other resources, and, in some cases, access to tutors who will answer questions sent in by email. Here are a few of the most useful sites:

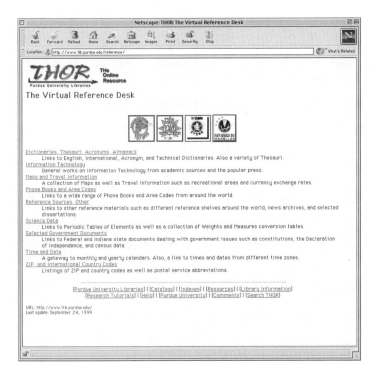

This page from Purdue University's virtual reference desk illustrates the many general reference materials that can be easily accessed online.

Screen capture courtesy of Purdue University Libraries.

Purdue University On-Line Writing Lab
owl.english.purdue.edu

- is the largest and most comprehensive of online writing labs
- offers 130 handouts on a wide variety of writing-related topics and links to scores of other sites, ranging from other writing centres to specialty search engines and reference collections
- presents current, concise information on citation in MLA and APA styles

Gayle Morris Sweetland Writing Center
www.lsa.umich.edu/swc/help/resources.html

- provides a collection of links to well-chosen reference materials

Utah Valley State College OWL
www.uvsc.edu/owl

- contains links to research tools, writing and grammar resources, and ESL information

There are also a number of sites that focus specifically on English usage, offering information on grammar, punctuation, style, format, errors commonly made by non-native speakers, and so on.

Resources for Writers and Writing Instructors
andromeda.rutgers.edu/~jlynch/Writing/links.html

Online Resources for Writers
webster.commnet.edu/writing/writing.htm

Advice on Academic Writing
www.utoronto.ca/writing/advise.html

The University of Victoria's Hypertext Writer's Guide
web.uvic.ca/wguide

Chapter 3

Managing Information

EVALUATING INTERNET SOURCES

One of the Internet's great strengths is also, for the researcher, one of its greatest hazards: its accessibility. The fact that there are almost no controls on the Internet and that anyone can gain access to it is exciting and genuinely revolutionary, but it is problematic for people who are trying to evaluate the information they find there. Students who, for example, consult a book from their library published by a well-known university press can safely assume that the material in it was subjected to some fairly rigorous quality controls in the course of its production and that it was chosen from among many others for the library's collection by a knowledgeable librarian. However, this is not the case with many sites on the Internet, which has no standards, no gatekeepers (like editors or librarians), and few enforceable rules. It is worthwhile to keep this in mind when perusing Web sites and to ask yourself a few questions:

1 Who is the author and/or the sponsor of the site?

- Does the site appear under the auspices of a reputable academic or other institution?
- Is the author (if he or she is identified) someone whose authority you can assess or confirm?

2 Is the site professionally presented?
- Is the writing well edited and free of errors?
- Is the site well organized and well designed?

3 Is the site intended for the scholar or for the general reader?
- Is the text at a high academic level? Does the author have knowledge of, and make use of, other important sources within the discipline?
- Is adequate documentation supplied?
- How does this resource compare with others that are available to you in other formats?

4 Can factual material be verified elsewhere?
- Are there places, on the Web or elsewhere, where you could go to confirm important facts or statistics?

5 What kind of links are provided?
- Are they evaluated or annotated?
- Do they lead to academic material or to sites intended for the entertainment of the general public?

6 Is the site recent or recently revised?
- Is someone keeping the site current, or has it been installed and then abandoned?

BOOKMARKS

Bookmarks (also called "Favourites") enable you to go directly to Web pages without inputting their addresses every time. A list of bookmarks is essentially an address book/speed-dialler composed of URLs. It is a good idea to get in the habit of bookmarking useful sites while you are visiting them. (Check your browser software for the easiest way to add bookmarks to your list.) Your bookmark list will probably grow at an alarming rate, requiring you to do some tidying up periodically; it helps to organize related bookmarks in folders (e.g., search engines, specialized directories on a particular topic), delete ones that cease to be relevant to your work, and alphabetize the rest.

Bookmarks can be saved to a disk; this is particularly useful if more than one person uses your computer or if you use more than one computer. It is also a good idea in terms of security; bookmarks can be accidentally deleted, and they can sometimes degrade. Some browsers allow you to make your bookmarks your home page, which is useful if you find yourself always beginning searches with them.

PRINTING AND SAVING ONLINE INFORMATION

When conducting research on the Internet, it is a good idea to print something from every source you consult. One reason for doing so is that online resources are inherently unstable—you could try to access the material again at a later date and discover that it has moved, has been revised, or has disappeared altogether. Another reason is that the printout from a Web site usually includes a record of your date of access and of the site's URL, two pieces of information you will require if you later need to cite the page as a source in any kind of bibliographic entry. As many people have discovered through bitter experience, computers are rather less tolerant of minor variations in an address than are human letter carriers; if the tiniest of details is incorrect or unclear in a handwritten transcript of a URL, it is totally useless.

KEEPING UP

The vastness of the Internet and its unprecedented rate of growth make it impossible to keep up with. What you can do, however, is stay reasonably up to date in one or two special areas of interest. Online groups like chats, newsgroups, and listservs can help. Many search engines and directories have a "what's new" feature or a "site of the week"; from the main menu of Yahoo!, this could be anything, but from a particular subject page of Infomine, for example, it might well be of interest to you. Sites that are devoted to tracking what's new on the Internet include:

Internet Resources Newsletter
www.hw.ac.uk/libWWW/irn/irn.html
- issues a monthly newsletter with an academic focus
- includes a library of notable recent sites

Scout Report

scout.cs.wisc.edu

- provides a guide to new resources, with an academic focus
- produces twice-monthly compilations organized by subject area, which provide summaries of new sites and links to them
- offers separate Scout Reports for Business and Economics, Science and Engineering, and Social Sciences

Research Buzz

www.researchbuzz.com

- presents "news and information about search engines and databases"
- offers a newsletter of Internet developments and emerging resources
- contains a searchable archive

Chapter 4

Citing
Internet
Sources

As a result of the ever-increasing variety of types and formats of information online, rules for citing Internet material are a bit unstable. Keep these few general notions in mind no matter which format you are using:

- Follow, as far as possible, your particular format's rules for citation of an equivalent or similar print source (in terms of ordering of elements, punctuation, etc.), adding and omitting elements as the situation demands.

- Remember that the whole point of citation is to enable your reader to locate and consult the source you have used; in the absence of the traditional features of a print source, such as an author's name or pagination, provide the data necessary to fully identify your online source and lead your reader efficiently to it.

- Provide date of posting or revision, and date of access—these dates are important in citing Internet sources because of the instability of online material.

- When in doubt, provide more specifying information, not less.
- Be consistent.

MLA STYLE

The following information is based on the fifth edition of the *MLA Handbook for Writers of Research Papers*, published in 1999, the first to incorporate the many revisions to its style rules that the Internet has occasioned. The MLA Web site (**www.mla.org**) also provides an exhaustive guide to citation of online material.

Because online information lacks standards of organization and because it is inherently unstable, entries referring to online sources need to include kinds of information that those referring to other media do not. The MLA recommends that Works Cited entries for online sources should contain whichever of the following categories of information are available and relevant (and in this order):

- name of author or site owner, or name of compiler, translator, or editor, followed by the abbreviation *ed., trans.,* or *comp.* (last name first)
- title of a short work within a database, site, or scholarly project (such as the name of an article or a story), in quotation marks
- title of a book, project, database or periodical; or, for a site with no title, a description such as *Home page* (underlined or italicized)
- name of editor, compiler, or translator (if not mentioned earlier), preceded by the abbreviation Ed., Trans., or Comp.
- publication information for any print version
- identifying numbers, such as version, volume and issue, or other
- date of posting or revision
- name of subscription service, name and location of library
- name of discussion list or forum
- name of any sponsoring institution
- for a journal, number range or total number of pages or paragraphs (if they are numbered)
- date of your access to the site

- complete URL (in angle brackets); if it has to be divided between two lines, it must be broken at a slash, with no hyphen.

CITATION MODELS

Web Page

Author's Last Name, First Name. *Title of Page*. Date of Posting or Revision. Date of Access. <URL>.

Online Journal Article

Author's Last Name, First Name. "Title of Article." *Title of Journal* Volume. Issue (Year): Pages or Paragraphs. Date of Access <URL>.

Electronic Correspondence

Author's Last Name, First Name. "Subject line." Email to the author. Date.

EXAMPLES OF MLA STYLE

Professional Site

Douglas Coupland Page. U of Guelph. 5 Feb. 2002 <http://www.coupland.uguelph.ca>.

Article in a Journal

Friser, Ingram. "The Suicide of Christopher Marlowe." *New Renaissance Studies* 1.3 (1998): 18 pars. 29 Dec. 1999 <http://newren.queensu.ca/index/html>.

Personal Site

Fraser, Iain. Home Page. 28 Feb. 2003 <http://www.inst.regello.it/776>.

Posting to a Discussion List

Bell, Sandra. "James I and Flyting." Online posting. 31 Jan. 2000 Scottish Renaissance Electronic Conference. 1 Mar. 2000 <http://scotrencon.utoronto/english-txt>.

Scholarly Project

Prison for Women Project. Ed. Austin Lowe. Nov. 1997. McGill U. 22 Aug. 2002 <http://www.mcgill.ca/P4W/~help>.

Book

Robertson, Bob. *In the Pink House.* [Toronto, 1995.] Prison for Women Project. Ed. Austin Lowe. Nov. 1997. McGill U. 22 Aug. 1998 <http://www.mcgill.ca/P4W/~help/robertson/html>.

Article in a Reference Database

"Jack Bush." *Encyclopedia Britannica Online.* Vers. 98.1. April 1998. Encyclopedia Britannica. 16 Apr. 2003 <http://www.britannica.com:700>.

   In parenthetical references in your text, cite Web sources like printed sources. One important common difference between the two types of sources is that Web documents are rarely paginated; if the paragraphs are numbered, cite them, using the abbreviation *pars*: "(Ireland, pars. 12–14)." Parenthetical references exist to guide your reader unequivocally to the relevant entry on your Works Cited page; provide what information you have accordingly. There is further advice on this topic, and on the citation of other sorts of sources, at the MLA Web site.

APA STYLE

The following information is based on the fifth edition of the *Publication Manual of the American Psychological Association* (2001), which provides extensive advice on the citation of online material of different kinds, and on material found at the APA Web site (www.apa.org).

CITATION MODELS

Web Site

Author's Last Name, First Initial or First Two Initials. (Year of Posting or Revision). *Title of work.* Retrieved month day, year from URL.

Online Journal

Author's Last Name, First Initial or First Two Initials. (Year of Publication). Title of article. *Title of Journal*, Volume or Number, Pages or Paragraphs. Retrieved month day, year from URL.

Electronic Correspondence

Email is considered a personal communication and so does not appear in a list of references. This is also true of other online sources that cannot be universally accessed, such as listservs.

EXAMPLES OF APA STYLE

Web Site with an Author

Hurst, G. (1998). *Drugs and repressed memory recovery*. Retrieved November 30, 1999, from http://www.psychstan.org/lpage.html.

Web Site with No Author

Electronic reference formats recommended by the American Psychological Association (2000). Washington, D.C.: American Psychological Association. Retrieved September 2, 2001, from http://www.apa.org/journals/webref.html.

Online Journal

Babcock, F. (1997). Gender issues in early education. *Journal of Psychological Research*, 4, 11 pars. Retrieved June 12, 2001, from http://www.jpsychr.edu/bbc2.htm.

Article from an Electronic Database

Flanagan, R. (1999). New e-commerce models. *New Brunswick Business Journal*, 11, pp. 58+. Retrieved March 1, 2001 from EBSCO database.

The standard parenthetical citation within a text includes the author's last name and the date of publication (to which is added a page reference if your citation refers to a direct quotation). This format is the starting point for a similar citation of an online source. If there is no author given, you may use the title (or a word or phrase from it that clearly identifies the source); if there is no page number, supply a paragraph number, if available, using either the "¶" symbol or the abbreviation "para." If no paragraph numbers are provided on the site, provide a heading from within the document and the number of the paragraph following it: (Neurological disorders, 2000, Conclusion, para. 2)

CBE STYLE

The seventh edition of *Scientific Style and Format: The CBE Manual for Authors, Editors, and Publishers* is appearing in 2003. The CBE currently recommends use of the National Library of Medicine guidelines for citation of online sources.

CITATION MODELS

Web Page

Author's Last Name First Initial Any Middle Initial. Date of Web Publication. Title of page. <URL>. Accessed Year Month Day.

Online Journal

Author's Last Name First Initial Any Middle Initial. Date of Publication. Title of article. In Title of Journal. Volume Number (Issue Number): Pages. <URL>. Accessed Year Month Day.

Electronic Correspondence

Author's Last Name First Initial Any Middle Initial. Title or subject line [email]. Message to: Receiver's name. Date and time of message [cited Date of Access]. [Length of message (screens, paragraphs, or lines)].

EXAMPLES OF CBE STYLE

Web Site

Johnson D. 2001. Anomalies in genome mapping. <http://www.genomearch.ca>. Accessed 2003 Feb 8.

Online Journal

Harvey P. 2001 May. New uses of allyl metal reagents. In Chemistry Q Online 23 (2). <http://www.chemq.org/rsc.html>. Accessed 2003 Jan 8.

Electronic Correspondence

Rosen J. Phylogenies [email]. Message to: Glen Sanderson. 2002 Dec 2, 11:40 am [cited 2003 March 22]. [about 3 screens].

Because of the present fluidity of citation formats and the relatively slow pace at which new developments find their way into print, the Internet itself is the best source for keeping abreast of revisions.

WEB SITES CONTAINING CITATION INFORMATION

MLA STYLE

MLA Style
www.mla.org
- is the official site of the Modern Languages Association
- contains sample entries for online citation, FAQs, and links to other MLA sites

A Guide for Writing Research Papers
webster.commnet.edu/mla/index.shtml
- provides an extensive guide to using MLA format for both online and print resources

Using MLA Format
owl.english.purdue.edu/handouts/research/r_mla.html
- presents models and examples of both print and online citations

APA STYLE

Electronic Reference Formats
www.apastyle.org/elecref.html
- provides format suggestions and a small collection of examples from the APA

Using APA Format
owl.english.purdue.edu/handouts/research/r_apa.html
- presents models and examples of both print and online citations

CBE STYLE

Online!: A Reference Guide to Using Internet Sources
www.smpcollege.com/online-4styles~help
- supplies extensive samples of CBE entries

Research and Documentation Online
www.dianahacker.com/resdoc/sciences/reference.html
- provides samples of CBE reference list entries and manuscript format

Chapter 5

A List of Useful Sites by Discipline

This chapter contains addresses of subject-specific directories that will lead you to information on whatever precise sub-topic you are exploring. But first, a few reliable basic directories that are of benefit to students in almost all subject areas:

Yahoo!
www.yahoo.com

Virtual Library
www.vlib.org

Internet Public Library
www.ipl.org

Infomine
infomine.ucr.edu

Librarians' Index to the Internet
lii.org

The relevant subject pages of these directories are always good starting places for online research, as they provide links to specialized directories and divide the broad subject into subcategories.

ACCOUNTING

Pro2Net
www.pro2net.com
- is a U.S. commercial site (formerly AccountingNet)
- offers search by keyword and topic and includes a research section that provides access to tax, budget, and financial data
- features on its home page a collection of recent accounting-related articles and news stories
- provides information on financial services, human resources, and insurance

Canadian Financial Network
www.canadianfinance.com/cfnbase/cdnbase.htm#Accountants
- provides an annotated list of Canadian and other accounting sites

RAW (Rutgers Accounting Web)
raw.rutgers.edu
- is one of the largest accounting Web sites on the Internet
- features a keyword search and links to associations, directories, and other resources

CPAnet
www.cpalinks.com
- includes up-to-date accounting-related news
- provides links to information on finance, tax and law, audit, and other related topics

Accounting Education.com
www.accountingeducation.com

- contains news, reviews, and a "book of the week" feature
- includes a database of accounting journals
- provides a collection of links to accounting resources

Canadian Institute of Chartered Accountants
www.cica.ca/cica/cicawebsite.nsf/public/homepage
- presents news related to accounting in Canada and elsewhere
- provides links to Canadian and international organizations

Social Science Information Gateway–Accounting
sosig.ac.uk/business/accounting_profession
- lists Internet resources by type (data, journals, mailing lists, etc.)
- emphasizes British and European information, but contains international links

Anet
www.csu.edu.au/anet
- contains links to research resources, mailing lists, and international organizations
- includes a business encyclopedia and an accounting bibliography

AccountingWeb
www.accountingweb.co.uk
- offers The Internet Monitor, a collection of annotated new links
- features The Accounting Web Internet Search Engine
- includes current accounting-related news stories

CPA Online
www.cpaonline.com
- has a catalog of over 300 accounting-related Web sites
- provides current and archived accounting news

Nelson's Accounting Web Site
accounting.nelson.com
- provides links to other accounting- and business-related sites

- offers numerous resource links, including information about educational opportunities, career planning, references and study resources, as well as an index of professional accounting firms worldwide

ANTHROPOLOGY

AnthroTECH

vlib.anthrotech.com

- is the anthropology home page of the Virtual Library
- provides links arranged by sub-topic and type of resource
- includes a "site of the day" and a "site of the month"

Academic Info: Anthropology

www.academicinfo.net/anth.html

- features a wide-ranging, up-to-date directory with annotated entries
- includes links to other directories, reference materials, museums, publications, and resources on many topics within anthropology

Anthropology Internet Resources

www.wcsu.ctstateu.edu/socialsci/antres.html

- offers general resources and links to sites on physical anthropology, archaeology, linguistics, Native Americans, culture, and sociology

Canadian Anthropology Society

socserv2.socsci.mcmaster.ca/~casca

- contains information on the society, news, and links to other Web resources

UCSB Department of Anthropology Links Directory

www.anth.ucsb.edu/links/pages

- contains more than 500 links arranged by topic and by region
- provides links to journals, museums, universities, organizations, conferences, course syllabuses, and field schools

LSU Libraries Webliography: Anthropology
www.lib.lsu.edu/soc/anthro.html
- provides an all-purpose directory with especially good reference links

Search Engines and Directories Limited to Archaeology and Anthropology
www.smsu.edu/contrib/library/resource/anthsrch.html
- provides links to search tools and information on specific topics, with an emphasis on antiquity

Anthro.Net
www.anthro.net
- contains a searchable database of reviewed Web sites and bibliographic references
- provides subject-specific links to online and print resources

Scholarly Societies Project—Anthropology
www.lib.uwaterloo.ca/society/anthrop_soc.html
- originates from the University of Waterloo
- presents links to international anthropological societies

UR-LIST: Web Resources for Visual Anthropology
www.usc.edu/dept/elab/urlist/index.html
- cross-indexes 375 anthropological sites according to the categories of information they contain

Humbul Humanities Hub – Archaeology
www.humbul.ac.uk/output/subout.php?subj=archaeology
- provides links to primary and secondary sources in archaeology and anthropology
- reviews new Web sites and academic information in the field

Consult also the anthropology pages at Voice of the Shuttle (vos.ucsb.edu)

BUSINESS

@brint.com
www.brint.com/interest.html

- features an extensive commercial directory with links to information on all business topics, including material on e-commerce, virtual corporations, intranets, and MIS (management information systems) research

Global Edge
globaledge.msu.edu/ibrd/ibrd.asp

- provides a well-organized collection of links to country information, periodicals, government resources, international trade information, and statistics
- includes a glossary of international business terms

Web Resources for International Economics and Business
Dylee.keel.econ.ship.edu/econ

- focuses on international trade, finance, development, management, marketing, accounting, and trade law
- provides links to statistics and institutions

Enterweb
www.enterweb.org/welcome.htm

- describes itself as "the knowledge portal for small business"
- focuses on micro-, small-, and medium-scale enterprises, cooperatives, and community economic development

Nelson's Business Communication Web Site
buscomm.nelson.com

- provides links to newspapers and magazines, job and career resources, Canadian associations essential to business communicators, and Canadian online writing labs for tips and guidance
- also gives links to useful reference resources such as online business directories and annual reports, government sources, ethics and legal information, and online dictionaries and encyclopedias

Business 2.0
www.business2.com
- features current business news, including market news from CNNMoney and technology news from CNET
- offers an extensive directory of business links

Business.com
www.business.com
- bills itself as "the business search engine"
- offers keyword search of the "business Internet" and a directory

Business-Related Search Engines
www.laisha.com/business.html
- contains links to specialized search engines and directories, under subheadings such as general business, accounting and finance, small business, and specialty businesses

Biz/ed
www.bized.ac.uk
- includes a directory of Internet business resources with 2200 links
- offers a collection of learning materials, statistics, and company facts

Consult also the online editions of business magazines:

Canadian Business
www.canadianbusiness.com

Report on Business Magazine
www.robmagazine.com

The Financial Post
www.nationalpost.com/financialpost

CRIMINOLOGY

U of T Centre of Criminology WWW Links
www.library.utoronto.ca/libraries_crim/centre/links.htm

- presents an excellent, exhaustive collection of links
- helpfully annotates most links and identifies Canadian links

National Criminal Justice Reference Service

www.ncjrs.org

- provides links to U.S. Web sites, databases, listservs, and other resources, including international resources
- includes topics such as drugs and crime, criminal justice statistics, juvenile justice, research, victims, and courts

Access to Justice Network

www.acjnet.org

- presents a collection of Canadian justice and legal information
- provides links to legislation, publications, databases, discussion groups, and organizations
- includes links to information on Aboriginal peoples, crime prevention, women, and youth

Florida State University School of Criminology Criminal Justice Links

www.criminology.fsu.edu/cjlinks

- includes both U.S. and international links on topics such as international criminal justice sources, civil liberties, pornography, juvenile delinquency, and police resources, maintained by Dr. Cecil Greek
- provides a good starting place for research on U.S. criminology

Canadian Comprehensive Criminology

www.paralegal.canlaw.net

- contains more than 2000 links related to Canadian criminal justice
- includes links to information on Canadian law, policing, prisons, statistics, and aboriginal issues

Cybrary

talkjustice.com/cybrary.asp

- created by criminology textbook author Dr. Frank Schmalleger
- offers Canadian and international links and a "Top 100 Picks" listing

Mega-links in Criminal Justice

faculty.ncwc.edu/toconnor

- provides annotated links to academically oriented sites, including the pages of many criminology professors
- offers general and subject-specific listings and a "top ten" collection

Department of Justice

canada.justice.gc.ca

- provides Department of Justice information and links to Canadian legal resources

Criminal Justice

cjwww.csustan.edu/cj/rframe.html

- this site, from California State University in Stanislaus, offers mostly American information on a wide range of criminology-related topics

Nelson's Criminology Web Site

criminology.nelson.com

- features links to the latest news affecting criminal justice and crime policy, as well as current criminal investigations, trials, and other incidents
- provides onsite resources and links to universities, conferences, associations, information for related careers, and essay writing and research resources

ENGLISH

eserver.org

eserver.org

- features one of the largest collections of humanities resources on the Web
- lists more than 30 000 works in art, architecture, drama, fiction, poetry, history, political theory, cultural studies, philosophy, women's studies, and music
- includes online journals, bulletin boards, and other resources

Voice of the Shuttle
vos.ucsb.edu

- provides an extensive, well-organized Web page of humanities resources
- offers directories by period, genre, and topics such as theory and minority literatures

Literary Resources on the Net
andromeda.rutgers.edu/~jlynch/Lit

- offers both keyword search and a selection of directory topics by period and topic
- lists extensive resources on U.S. literature

Humbul Humanities Hub
www.humbul.ac.uk

- is operated by Oxford University (originated at Bath University in the mid-1980s)
- allows users to search its own database or the Web
- provides links to many journals and other online literary resources

Louisiana State University Libraries Webliography: Literature
www.lib.lsu.edu/hum/lit-main.html

- provides a list of mostly reference links, including literary bibliographies, style guides, and electronic texts

Contemporary Philosophy, Critical Theory and Postmodern Thought
carbon.cudenver.edu/~mryder/itc_data/postmodern.html

- offers an extensive collection of links to information on critics, schools of thought, and issues in contemporary literary theory

MIT Libraries—Literature Resources
libraries.mit.edu/guides/subjects/literature/index.html

- offers a collection of links organized by period, nationality, and genre

Internet Public Library

www.ipl.org

- contains the Online Literary Criticism Collection of more than 2500 Web sites indexed by author, title, and period, in addition to its many useful reference resources

University of Connecticut—English and American Literature Resources

www.lib.uconn.edu/subjectareas/engweb.html

- presents annotated links to etext collections, author sites, and other information, arranged by period

A Literary Index—Internet Resources in Literature

www.vanderbilt.edu/AnS/english/flackcj/Litmain.html

- an extensive descriptive meta-index of literary resources, links, and collections
- includes information on rhetoric, research, and etext archives

Nelson's English Resource Centre

http://englishresources.nelson.com

- includes a glossary of literary terms, a guide to MLA documentation, and a collection of links to sites containing primary sources, information on individual authors, and theory
- offers information on business and technical communication

Note: For more information on communications, see also www.communicate.nelson.com

ENVIRONMENTAL SCIENCE

Environment Canada's Green Lane

www.ec.gc.ca

- supplies information about Environment Canada and other government agencies, plus links to newsletters, publications, and related sites

Envirolink Network

envirolink.netforchange.com

- offers searches by keyword and links organized into categories such as events, publications, government resources, and organizations
- provides a compendium of recent environmental news stories, many from an activist perspective

Best Environmental Directories
www.ulb.ac.be/ceese/meta/cds.html
- aims to provide "the best starting point for each subject"
- indexes more than 600 environmental subjects
- originates in Belgium and is especially strong on Europe-related information

Amazing Environmental Organization Web Directory
www.webdirectory.com
- provides links by topic and access to newsgroups, databases, and government information
- bills itself as "the Earth's Biggest Environmental Search Engine"

Academic Info: Environmental Studies
www.academicinfo.net/environst.html
- features an up-to-date, all-purpose, independent directory with annotated links
- provides access to other directories, reference materials, databases and archives, libraries, and publications

EnviroInfo
www.deb.uminho.pt/fontes/enviroinfo
- is based in Portugal
- provides links to more than 700 journals

WWW Virtual Library: Environment
earthsystems.org/virtuallibrary/vlhome.html
- provides links to sites that focus on biodiversity, environmental law, oceanography, sustainable development, and other environmental issues

Environment Web Resources
www.herts.ac.uk/lis/subjects/natsci/env/envweb/index.html
- is produced by the University of Hertfordshire
- provides an extensive list of Web resources divided into 25 subjects, with annotated links

Nelson's Environmental Studies Web Site
environment.nelson.com
- includes an EnviroUpdates section, which provides the latest news on the environment
- provides links related to education and careers and also links to environmental listservs, newsgroups, and Canadian environmental organizations

HUMAN RESOURCE MANAGEMENT

HR On-Line
www.hronline.com
- offers current news, Canadian statistics, and links to sites on a variety of HR topics

Human Resources Development Canada
www.hrdc-drhc.gc.ca
- provides information from and about the government agency, including news releases and speeches, labour market information, guides to programs and services, and links to other resources

HR OnLINE
www.hr2000.com/main.asp
- offers search by keyword and a directory that includes assessment tools, best practices, compensation and benefits, training and development, career services, and software

The Human Resource Professional's Gateway to the Internet
www.hrprosgateway.com/www/index2.html
- includes a keyword search, live chat, and a collection of annotated links

HR-Guide.com
www.HR-Guide.com
- is part of the HR webring
- provides a large collection of links organized by topic
- includes a "featured Website" link

HR Zone
www.hrzone.com
- features information on hiring, firing, workers' compensation, discrimination, and law, as well as links to new research, newsletters, and other Web resources

Society for Human Resources Management Online
www.shrm.org
- provides information on the society and recent HRM news
- includes links to conferences, publications, listservs, newsgroups, and other online resources
- offers a collection of articles on current HR issues, keyword search, and a list of featured links

HR-Guide.Com
www.hr-guide.com
- contains links to other Internet-based resources for HR professionals and students
- offers a wide-ranging directory and a "New This Month" feature

Nelson's Human Resource Management Web Site
hrm.nelson.com
- provides links to sites on labour economics, training and development, strategic planning, compensation, and other HR issues

POLITICAL SCIENCE

Canadian Politics on the Internet
www.library.ubc.ca/poli/cpweb.html

- provides an extensive collection of resources on Canadian politics, government, public policy, and related topics

Social Science Information Gateway—Politics

sosig.ac.uk/roads/subject-listing/World-cat/politics.html

- is an excellent source for information on British and international politics
- provides an annotated list of resources
- contains the full texts of many articles, papers, and reports

Political Science Resources on the Web

www.lib.umich.edu/govdocs/poliscinew.html

- supplies a wide-ranging collection of international links with a particular emphasis on U.S. politics

Richard Kimber's Political Science Resources

www.psr.keele.ac.uk

- features a well-organized collection of links presented by a professor at the University of Keele, England
- is especially strong on political theory and thought, British politics, and international relations

Canadian Political Science Association

www.cpsa-acsp.ca

- contains information relating to the association itself and links to journals, other associations, universities, and some general Internet sources

Academic Info: Political Science

www.academicinfo.net/polisci.html#foreign

- supplies an independently compiled, annotated directory of Internet resources
- includes meta-indexes, reference materials, and links on a wide variety of topics, including Canadian and U.S. politics, Marxism, anarchism, and church–state issues

Political Science Research Resources

www.vanderbilt.edu/~rtucker/polisci

- provides links to resources on standard political science topics and information on dynamic models, artificial intelligence, game theory, and econometrics

Political Resources on the Net
www.politicalresources.net

- provides listings of political sites sorted by country, with links to parties, organizations, governments, and media

PolitInfo.com
politinfo.com

- this "independent, non-partisan portal for political resources, news, and information" contains a wide-ranging directory with links to more than 10 000 sites, current news stories, and information on books and other publications

Nelson's Political Science Web Site
polisci.nelson.com

- offers a collection of political documents, news features, and links to information on Canadian and introductory government and politics

▆▆▆▆▆▆ PSYCHOLOGY

Psychology Online Resource Central
www.psych-central.com

- provides a well-maintained set of links to reference materials, journals, newsgroups, libraries, organizations, directories, and many other resources

American Psychological Association
www.apa.org

- contains information on the organization's activities and publications, new research, conferences, citation styles, and related materials

AmoebaWeb
www.vanguard.edu/faculty/ddegelman/amoebaweb

- provides links to information on all the branches of psychology, under headings such as full-text journals, study skills, research methods, statistical analysis, and professional organizations
- includes an archive of featured Web sites

Psych Web
www.psywww.com
- offers links to scholarly resources, books, academic departments, and journals
- also includes quizzes, career information, and links to self-help resources

PsychCrawler
www.psychcrawler.com
- is produced by the American Psychological Association
- offers a psychology search engine that indexes a growing collection of Web sites, including the APA site

Psychological Research on the Net
psych.hanover.edu/Research/exponnet.html
- provides a list of links to current research arranged by subject

Encyclopedia of Psychology
www.psychology.org
- offers keyword search and a directory-style subject tree leading to articles on particular topics and links to related sites

PsychScholar
psych.hanover.edu/Krantz
- provides links to reference resources, journals, associations, and software

Nelson's Psychology Web Site
psychology.nelson.com
- features links to psychology resources on the Web, including searchable databases, journals, and reference materials

SOCIOLOGY

SocioWeb

www.socioweb.com/~markbl/socioweb

- bills itself as "Your Independent Guide to Sociological Research on the Internet"
- offers keyword search and links to associations, journals and magazines, university departments, statistics, and other indexes and guides

Social Science Information Gateway: Sociology

www.sosig.ac.uk/sociology

- features a wide-ranging set of links to international resources
- includes subsections on the sociology of gender and sexuality, economics, education, law and crime, medicine, politics, sport, race and ethnicity, work, family, and the elderly

A Sociological Tour through Cyberspace

www.trinity.edu/~mkearl/index.html#in

- presents a playful, helpful introduction to online sociological materials, containing a well-organized body of links arranged by topic
- includes both standard sociological topics and more eccentric choices such as paranormal sites and health statistics and the medical establishment

SocioSite

www.pscw.uva.nl/sociosite/index.html

- includes links to listservs, newsgroups, data archives, research centres, and other resources, from the University of Amsterdam

Academic Info: Sociology

www.academicinfo.net/soc.html

- provides usefully annotated links to reference material, discussion groups, and online journals and newsletters
- includes pages on Durkheim, gay and lesbian studies, religious movements, and economics

Sociology: A Guide to Internet Resources
www2.lib.udel.edu/subj/soc/internet.htm
- offers an extensive, well-maintained set of links from the University of Delaware Library
- presents links grouped under headings including social issues, theory, associations and organizations, and discussion groups and mailing lists

Dead Sociologists' Society
www2.pfeiffer.edu/~lridener/DSS/DEADSOC.HTML
- provides information on many major sociological thinkers
- offers links arranged by subject

Statistical Resources on the Web: Sociology
www.lib.umich.edu/libhome/Documents.center/stsoc.html
- provides access to statistical materials on hundreds of subjects

Nelson's Sociology Web Site
sociology.nelson.com
- includes a wide assortment of links and resources on sociology, social issues, and glossaries, as well as links to information about degrees and careers

Consult also:
- The Sociolog (**www.sociolog.com**)
- Internet Crossroads in the Social Sciences (**dpls.dacc.wisc.edu/newcrossroads/ index.asp**)